CONVAIR XFY-1 "POGO"

INTRODUCTION:

In 1947 both the U. S. Air Force and the U. S. Navy sponsored VTOL design studies called Project Hummingbird. The rapid development of increasingly powerful powerplants had reached the point where a true VTOL aircraft was in the realm of possibility. The Air Force's motive came from its firsthand experiences in Europe at the end of World War Two. The U. S. Air Force had demonstrated how swiftly fixed airfields could be overrun. It was evident from this experience that any future war would be won or lost within the first twenty-four hours and the winner would accomplish this through the elimination of the loser's airfields. This vulnerability of fixed bases is what has made the U. S. Navy's carrier task force the politician's tool of choice to solve peacekeeping issues into the 1990s. However, the U. S. Navy's firsthand experiences with Japans Kamikaze taught them the vulnerability of their great mobile peacekeepers, the carrier. Because of this experience the Navy felt that the only way to protect any naval presence in enemy waters was to equip all ships with a VTOL fighter.

In 1948, the Navy organized a more formal study for a VTOL fighter based on information derived from project Hummingbird and from captured German documents pertaining to the Focke-Wulf Triebflugel VTOL ramjet fighter. The Navy's VTOL fighter was to be housed in a vertical tepee type structure aboard most all ships including the following: LST, fleet oiler, tender, transport, destroyer and larger capital ships. The new VTOL fighter would be launched once a radar threat was known and then be radar guided to intercept the attackers. This would provide the task force or convoy a mobile aerial picket line that in theory would hold the attackers at bay until carrier aircraft could arrive.

DEVELOPMENT:

On 31 May 1951 the Navy awarded both Convair and Lockheed contracts to develop the world's first VTOL fighters around the turboprop engine. Convair's XFY-1 and Lockheed's XFV-1 both were designed around the Allison YT-40 coupled engine. The YT-40 was created by marrying two T-38 turboprop engines into a single gearbox to drive the counter-rotating propellers. The T-40 [...] North American XA2J-1 "Super Savage" and the Convair R3Y-1/-2 "Tradewind" flying boats.

Even though the contracts called for two aircraft to be produced by each company only one each was completed. Armament was to be either two or four 20MM guns or forty-eight folding fin rockets located in wing tip pods, a feature never installed or tested. Wing

Dramatic rollout photo of the powerful XFY-1 "Pogo". (Convair via B. J. Long)

At Left, the Focke-Wulf "Triebflugel" was a German design study for a ramjet powered VTOL fighter. Above, the proof of concept engine test rig for the YT-40 engine. Below, the Convair XFY-1 "Pogo" on 3-15-54 during ground transporter tests prior to its shipment to NAS Moffett Field for tethered hangar tests. The transporter issue was not addressed by Lockheed. (USN)

tip and vertical tail pods also housed the four caster type landing gear on both companies designs.

From the start, Convair elected to operate the XFY-1 in the VTOL mode. The major factor for this decision was that no workable temporary landing

gear solution was deemed acceptable due to the Pogo's unique cruciform design combination of a delta wing plus large vertical and ventral fins. Since such a solution was available on the Lockheed XFV-1, Convair received the first suitable vertical running Allison YT-40. VTOL engine testing began in earnest in December 1953 when Convair started construction on a vertical test rig at Lindbergh Field, California. The rig consisted of the engine and its propellers and an abbreviated forward fuselage including the cockpit all fitted on four legs. The 5,850 SHP engine was up and running by February 1954 and was virtually trouble free. March saw the engine installed and the transporter/lifting cradle tested under the eyes of CAPT C. W. Sterling USN, the Bureau of Aeronautics representative.

After the initial engine test at Lindbergh Field, the engine and its airframe were shipped to NAS Moffett Field, California, for tethered flight testing. Convair took over the 195 foot high old rigid Airship Hangar Number One for this phase of the testing. This series of tethered flight tests were officially called "vertical taxi trials". 29 April 1954 saw Convair engineering test pilot James F. "Skeets" Coleman, LTCOL USMCR, make the first tethered flight. This would be followed by hundreds of takeoffs and landings culminating in a free vertical hover outside the hanger on 1 August 1954. On this first free hover an altitude of only 20 feet was achieved. On the next attempt the Pogo climbed to 150 feet before backing back down.

Convair engineers did an excellent job in designing a ground transporter for their VTOL aircraft. The "Pogo" is seen here being lifted into the vertical launch position on 3-15-54. (National Archives)

The aircraft was then shipped back to NAAS Brown Field, California, to conduct complete flight testing including transitions to horizontal flight. Starting in September, some seventy short vertical test hops were conducted by "Skeets" in preparation for his transition to horizontal flight and back again to vertical flight and landing. On 2 November the first transition to horizontal flight took place with 21 minutes of the 28 minute flight being in the horizontal. Two days later, on 4 November 1954, the world press and the U. S. military were invited to a public demonstration of this unique machine.

Flying the Navy AD-5 chase aircraft for the first two "Pogo" horizontal flights was LCDR Bergsted, a BuAer representative at Convair. With LCDR Bergsted in the AD-5 during the first flight was Convair test pilot B. J. Long (see Naval Fighters #23, Convair XF2Y-1 and YF2Y-1 SeaDart), candidate backup pilot for the "Pogo". A Navy HUP helicopter, from HU-1 at NAAS Ream Field, was present and airborne for the vertical flight tests and for the horizontal demonstrations. The AD-5 joined as chase for horizontal flights carrying technical observers and photographers.

These first two transitions to horizontal flight were executed in a beautiful and spectacular manner, as all of "Skeet's" later horizontal demonstrations. After vertical lift off, he smoothly transitioned to horizontal flight with no more than fifty feet under the vertical fin of the "Pogo-Stick". After horizontal passes over NAAS Brown Field, "Skeets" transitioned to vertical flight with a descent to a gentle spot touchdown like a ballet dancer. Convair personnel and invited guests were ecstatic with both of these initial horizontal flights of the powerful "Pogo" and the flying skill demonstrated by "Skeets".

After the 4 November Pogo demonstration, the dignitaries were transported to the Convair seaplane ramp on San Diego bay for further demonstrations of Convair test aircraft. The next demonstration was of the huge T-40 powered R3Y-1 Tradewind flying boat which was followed by the Convair SeaDart. The Sea Dart demonstration turned into a disaster when the number two aircraft broke up in flight (see Naval Fighters #23, the Convair XF2Y-1 and YF2Y-1 SeaDart) due to high a speed pitch oscillation, killing its pilot Chuck Richbourg.

From this point until termination of the "Pogo" project on 1 August 1956, sporadic testing was conducted. On 5 February 1955 "Skeets" took the Pogo to 10,000 feet for the first time. B. J. Long took over the SeaDart project with the death of Richbourg and John Knebel was named backup pilot. On 19 May Knebel attempted to fly the XFY-1 vertically at Lindbergh Field without rig training. The results were almost disastrous and the flight was terminated in a hard landing and the decision to set up the tether rig at NAAS Brown Field for the training of new pilots. "Skeets" made his final and longest flight on 16 June 1955. Tether rig training was resumed on 8 May 1956 with Charles E. "Chuck" Myers, Jr. and John Knebel. This went on for 32 days until 1 August, but no further flights were made. By this time conventional aircraft were approaching Mach-2 and most carrier related problems in operating jets at sea were resolved. In addition, the YT-40's gearbox had started making metal and would need to be overhauled. Since no more government money was forthcoming, the project was cancelled.

The aircraft stayed locally in the San Diego area for a few years before being shipped to NAS Norfolk where it stood as a gateguard until being stored at the NASM storage facility at Silverhill, Maryland.

Ejection seat tests were conducted on the "Pogo" prior to its shipment to NAS Moffett Field. The tests proved that the XFY-1 would have to be at an altitude of 200 feet to complete a successful ejection. The photo shows a dummy being ejected against a demarcated board for photographic clarity and better interpretation. "Skeets" Coleman made all his flights with the ejection seat unarmed. (National Archives)

FLYING CHASE
OBSERVATIONS BY CONVAIR ENGINEERING TEST PILOT B. J. LONG

CDR Billy Jack "B. J." Long USNR (RET) is a member of the Society of Experimental Test Pilots and graduate of the Navy Test Pilot School.

In the fall of 1954 I had been designated the potential back up pilot for the "Pogo". In December 1954, Convair test pilot John Knebel was assigned as the back up pilot when I took over the SeaDart program. Because of this I did not fly the XFY-1, but I did observe "Skeets" Coleman, the project engineering test pilot, make all the vertical and horizontal test flights from 1954 until well into 1955.

My observations were made from the ground and as chase pilot for the horizontal flights. As such I have personal opinions about the XFY-1 design features and apparent flight characteristics as reviewed in the following narration.

The Convair XFY-1 delta wing design was far superior to the Lockheed XFV-1 aircraft with its short span tapered wing. At very high angles of attack the delta wing had much better lift, stability, and control characteristics. The delta wing design provided the XFY-1 with a larger "footprint" than the XFV-1 on which to mount the four small landing gear. I also had the opportunity to observe Herman "Fish" Salmon, noted test pilot, fly the Lockheed XFY-1 at altitude where all the vertical and hovering tests took place. The takeoffs were all done with a very large fixed landing gear partially because the only vertically running J-40 was given to Convair.

The "Pogo" operated from and to the ground surface in the vertical regime; ie. as a "tail sitter" for the take off and landing. The aircraft had four full castering small wheels shock mounted at the tips of the wing and fins. No brakes were provided for the wheels, thus it was mandatory to flight test in a no wind condition. This wheel and no brake system would be completely unacceptable for operational use aboard ship or land base.

The "Pogo's" engine was one-of-a-kind and needed a special lubrication system for extended vertical operations. The engine demonstrated great power loss with rising ambient temperatures. Thus all flight tests were conducted in the early morning for lower temperature and no wind conditions. The coupled engine, gear box, and counterrotating propellers had low experience levels requiring

The Navy AD-5 (BuNo 133927) used by Convair pilots for chase and logistic flights supporting the XFY-1 "Pogo" and other Convair test aircraft. Convair test pilots John Knebel (left) and B. J. Long (R) pose with the AD-5 at NAAS Brown Field near the Mexican border, where "Pogo" flight tests were conducted. Note the large compartment aft of the cockpit that permitted photographers and technical observers for test flights. In early 1955 Knebel was designated "Pogo" back-up pilot. (B. J. Long)

constant inspection and maintenance. The propellers and exhaust in flight idle setting during horizontal flight created excessive thrust and resulting high airspeed such that "slow flight" was impossible. Aerodynamic speed brakes could not help slow down the XFY-1 because none were installed on the "Pogo". The "Pogo" was so fast at idle that while flying chase with our Navy AD-5, I had some difficultly maintaining a close formation position even using almost all of the engine's 2,500 HP. To my knowledge, "Skeets" never closed the canopy of the XFY-1 even during horizontal flight ---- and I don't blame him. I'm sure he didn't want any delays if he had to bail out.

Lift off and transition to horizontal flight appeared easy with smooth application of power and a gentle push over. "Skeets" had mastered this maneuver from the beginning. The return to vertical flight from horizontal flight, the hovering descent from altitude, and the final descent for touchdown including horizontal transition in the hovering mode to an exact spot landing was infinitely more difficult and dangerous.

To return from horizontal flight, "Skeets" would begin his transition maneuver flying as low as possible in horizontal flight, at idle power, across Brown Field. Arriving at the center of the field he would pull sharply into a vertical climb, still in idle power. The trick was to apply power at the peak of the climb as the "Pogo" stopped its vertical accent, thus acquiring vertical hovering flight. Then began the delicate task of vertical descent from sometimes well over 1,000 feet of altitude.

Once in the vertical hovering flight, the "Pogo" had no inherent stability on any axis. It was like sitting on a flagpole and trying to control ascent or descent with a very delicate touch on the throttle of the 5,850 shaft horsepower engine/propeller system.

At heights above several hundred feet in hovering flight, including vertical ascent or descent, pilots cannot judge low vertical velocities or even vertical directions when looking straight down at the ground. Helicopter pilots will verify this. Even now AV-8B "Harrier" pilots start vertical descent from about 75 feet.

However, "Skeets" had acquired the skill and technique to make these very difficult vertical descents from altitude. He and his XFY-1 flight test engineer, Bob McGeary, had developed a ground-based visual aid such that Bob could provide voice cues to "Skeets" during these vertical descents. At about 200 feet and below, "Skeets" always demonstrated his outstanding control for final descent to a spot landing.

The vertical descents visually revealed very rapid movement of all aerodynamic control surfaces: wing elevon plus upper and lower rudders. As the "Pogo" neared the ground surface, with the aircraft becoming enveloped in its own "prop wash" being deflected off the ground, control frequency seemed to increase, indicating positive and stable attitude control becoming more demanding. However, "Skeets", as usual, demonstrated his mastery of flying this monster.

It was obvious early in the program that inherent pilot skills and extensive flight experience were not enough to jump into the "Pogo" and fly it safely or effectively. "Skeets" many vertical tests in the tethered rig at Moffett Field and his many free flight vertical tests before committing to horizontal flight provided him with the additional skills and knowledge to demonstrate the VTOL "tail setter" concept safely.

For his efforts LTCOL James F. "Skeets" Coleman USMCR was presented the prestigious Harmon Award by the President of the United States for the XFY-1 test flights.

Preparations for the 11-4-54 press flight started with the launch of HUP helicopter on loan from HU-1 followed by B. J. Long in the AD-5 seen in the background. (National Archives)

FLYING THE CONVAIR XFY-1 "POGO"
BY PROJECT ENGINEERING TEST PILOT JAMES F. "SKEETS" COLEMAN

STABILITY PATTERN TESTING:

Prior to my tethered test flights at NAS Moffett's 195 foot high blimp hangar number one, I wanted to experience as many and varied stability patterns as possible. I was anticipating a unique stability pattern and wanted to be prepared to handle it. To prepare myself I received permission from the Navy to conduct stability tests on all the different types of helicopters assigned to NAAS Ream Field, San Diego.

Since at that time the project was secret, the Navy personnel were instructed not to ask what, as one LCDR put it, 'what the hell are you doing'. They were worried enough about my sanity, but when I took the seat out and laid flat on my back, they really went crazy. After flying all the helicopters available I suspected that I would have trouble with altitude. I had big arguments with the Navy pilots about landing without the ability to view the ground or use an altimeter. The argument was settled when I covered up their altimeter and made them attempt landings while looking straight ahead. They couldn't tell if they were going up or down and damn near killed themselves.

Because of the human element pilots sometimes tend to get into response with the moment of the airplane. At one point this happened to me in a Boeing Vertol. I got into a moment that became more and more exaggerated and I had to go against my instincts and do the opposite of what I felt. I had two Convair engineers looking over my shoulder saying 'hey "Skeets", bet you can't lick this one', and I was saying to myself, 'if you two dummies are right we are all dead'.

TETHERED FLIGHT TESTS:

We shipped the "Pogo" to NAS Moffett Field where we would be able to conduct tethered test flights in a no wind environment. We rigged the tether in hanger number one where I would be able to raise the XFY-1 at least 100 feet. The prop spinner was

---

The XFY-1 on its transporter in the blimp hanger at Moffitt Field with the engine and propeller removed. The cruciform tips are removed and a blade antennae is visible. (National Archives)

removed and a rig was installed above the propellers with a cable in a drum which could either lift me up or slack off to let me back down. However the devise did not allow enough slack to hit the propeller. For safety sake a protective ring was put around the cable just above the propellers. We removed the cruciform tips and attached cables to them that went to powered drums. If I called for help Bob McGeary could slap that thing and it would pull tight and straighten me right up. And I had to call him alot. My call was 'McGeary catch me -- catch me'. Because of this we were really worried about the project.

What we didn't realize was when

"Skeets" prepares for a tethered flight in June 1954. Note the cables attached to the four gear legs on the wing tips. (National Archives)

you fly in the hanger you created "wall effect". We were recirculating the air creating terrific turbulence which contributed to loss of control at zero airspeed while in a hover. I would get to twisting and turning and I couldn't control anything, so Bob would hit the lever snapping all the cables taunt.

When we figured out what was happening we took the "Pogo" out of the blimp hanger and I flew a couple of uneventful free hovers without the ill effects of the hanger turbulence.

We had made our first tethered flight at Moffett on 29 April 1954 and conducted our first free vertical hover at Moffett on 1 August.

"Skeets" hovers at about 50 feet during tethered flight tests on 6-14-54. Note tufting attached to the wings for the tests. (National Archives)

THE ALLISON YT-40 TURBOPROP ENGINE

The Allison YT-40 engine consisted of two smaller T-38s mounted in tandem, delivering their power through a single gearbox. These drove a pair of Curtiss-Wright turboelectric co-axial contra-rotating propellers sixteen feet in diameter. This was the only vertical running YT-40 engine delivered and developed an estimated 5,850 shaft horsepower.

PHOTOS: Below left, Convair engineers complete the final check of the YT-40 engine prior to installation in June 1954. Below, a Convair engineer makes a last minute inspection in September 1954 at NAAS Brown Field. These two photos illustrate the fact that the YT-40 was a plumber's nightmare. Top right, the XFY-1 on the transporter with the engine removed and the engine doors in the open position. The "Pogo" was built with ease-of-maintenance in mind. Bottom right, the YT-40 engine is being lowered into the engine bay of the XFY-1. Note the Convair engineer standing in the engine bay guiding the engine into position. (National Archives)

FLIGHT CHARACTERISTICS:

The takeoff and transition to horizontal flight was easy due to the tremendous power of the YT-40. The transition to horizontal flight was like taking a ski out of water and usually occurred at about fifty feet. However the return to vertical flight and its corresponding landing were a very different story altogether!

The airplane was very fast and you could hardly slow it down. It had no drag devices, no wheels, no flaps, no nothing. Even at flight idle it was too fast. I'd be tooling around up there with B. J. chasing me in his AD-5 and he would drop out of sight because he just couldn't keep up with me. Even when cut back to flight idle, I couldn't slow it down enough to make tight turns.

I came around the first time and we didn't know what would happen. All we knew was the delta wing wouldn't stall like a straight wing. A delta wing C_L Max curve goes up then straight across where as a straight wing's C_L Max curve goes up then drops off fast and the airplane goes into a spin. With the delta wing on the straight portion of the line, if you were to increase your rate of descent you

---

Below, "Skeets" Coleman enters the cockpit during a dry run prior to the first untethered flight at NAS Moffett Field. Note the aircraft is still hooked up to the transporter. (via B. J. Long)

would tumble. During model testing at NASA Langly I watched it tumble. This of course made me very careful because there was no way you can recover from a tumble, particularly if you were doing it close to the ground.

The first time I tried to land I had no idea it would be that fast. I couldn't slow the darn thing down so I just tightened up the turns and came around. When I got it tightened up enough I reduced the power and got close to the ground and popped up into the vertical. It would climb even at idle when I would first transition to the vertical. As the airplane climbed, the gain in altitude destroyed my depth perception because of the lack of movement across a reference point. This caused me to look over my shoulder to try and gage my position. The problem was no one had ever given me any aerodynamic predictions, so I had to feel it out. I tried to back down, but when I got down to between 300 and 500 feet I lost my depth perception and didn't know

Below, "Skeets" sets the "Pogo" down after it's first hover on 8-1-54. Note Convair insignia aft of the cockpit.. (National Archives)

Above, clad in "G" suit, sneakers and life jacket, "Skeets" Coleman climbs the ladder to the cockpit in preparation for the aircraft's first untethered liftoff at Moffett Field on 8-1-54. Below, the first hover. (National Archives)

what to do. On this first horizontal flight there were a few helicopters around chasing me. I called out to have them hover at 100 feet to give me a reference point because I had no idea whether I was going up or down. All I could tell was that I was vertical. I finally set the bird down, but the difficulties I encountered caused some the these big hiatuses (gap in time) between flights. We had to figure out a way to tell me whether I was descending or ascending.

Chuck Myers believed that you could judge your ascent or descent by looking over the wing, a notion that I

Below, the XFY-1 was returned to the San Diego area in September 1954 and continued vertical testing. Note that the lower vertical fin tip did not have its covering installed during these tests. (via B. J. Long)

didn't agree with. If you're looking over the wing, how do you remain perfectly vertical? If you don't remain perfectly vertical you would stub your fin or worse. If you did not maintain a straight and level attitude when you backed down you ran the risk of toppling over because of the aircraft's high center of gravity (CG). This would be true especially in a high wind condition. You also had to manipulate the propeller controls to give you some negative pitch, actually putting it into the beta regime so you could get some pressure on the oleos to press the airplane down. Of course I had control of the weather so we never went up in a high wind.

We did two things to remedy my landing problem after a long time and many conferences. We let a contract to Ryan Aeronautical and effectively put them into the doppler business. They designed a doppler for us which was mounted out on the left hand pod.

At right, vertical tests at NAAS Brown Field in September 1954. (National Archives)

The doppler had a gauge that I had to look at closely even though I was quite busy. The gauge, which was located on the back of the seat, was a rate of descent indicator which was a simple sensitive needle gauge. Because I could hardly keep my eyes off the ground, we put three lights (green, amber, red) on the left wing pod. Green = zero or positive ascent, am-

Below, the XFY-1 prepares for an engine test in October 1954 with five fire trucks at the ready. Bottom, on 10-2-54 Convair engineers install a strain gauge to the wing tip. (USN)

ber = going down safely, and red = unsafe. I believe red indicated more than a ten feet per second descent. So if the red light came on I would immediately have to add power and of course things were very slow in reacting. In a hover your control was strictly aerodynamic, so when you added power you had spin-up and thrust that were delayed but you had slipstream to have control.

The doppler was a qualitative cue not a quantitative cue, in that it provided me with the knowledge to keep me in what we considered a safe zone.

Lockheed adopted the doppler too, but it was only one of many changes they made which put their program behind ours.

To keep the airplane vertical required 3 to 4 degrees of trim. Even though the forces on the controls were artificial, it would require about three pounds of force per degree. This control displacement really got tiresome because you were laying on your back pressing up. A hover would require about 3 degrees nose-down trim to prevent the airplane from going over on its back. On take-off you required 3 to 4 degrees nose-up trim.

THE PILOT'S SEAT:

During takeoff and landing everything was happening at once. If your seat did not rotate during the transition you would literally fall out of the airplane, I don't care how strong you were or how tight your shoulder straps or seat belt were, you would fall out of the cockpit. However, it

At right, two views of the XFY-1 on the morning of 11-4-54 prior to its press flight. The large spinner above the propeller blades held a huge parachute to be deployed in case of engine failure in the vertical position. It would be ejected vertically above the propellers with enough height to avoid being sucked into the blades. Once deployed the parachute would hopefully save the aircraft. (via B. J. Long)

wasn't as bad on takeoff as you could manipulate the throttle. So in flight the seat was rotated back. On landing you rotated it forward so you wouldn't slide out head first. During the transition from vertical to horizontal or horizontal to vertical flight I had to accomplish two mechanical functions in addition to jockeying the normal flight controls

CONVAIR XFY-1 COCKPIT DETAILS

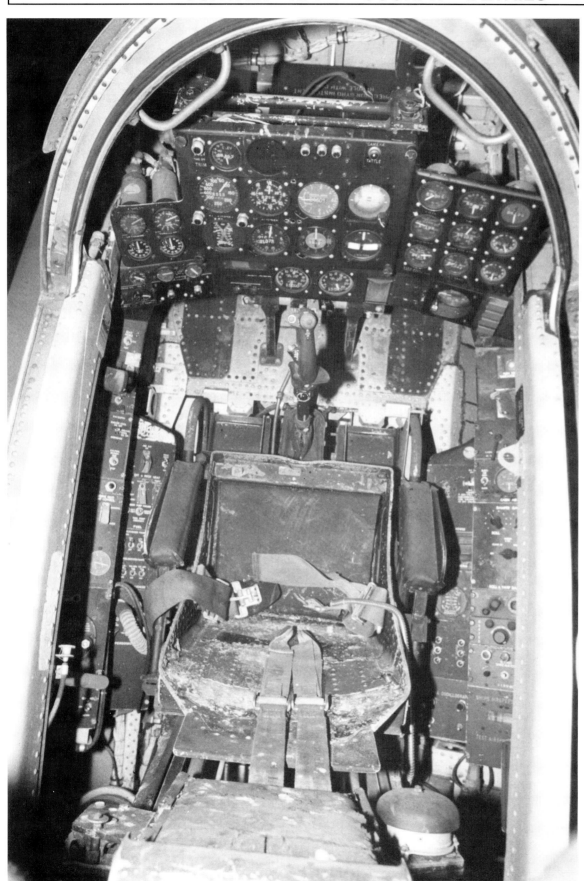

At left, utilitarian cockpit of the XFY-1 "Pogo". The seat was rigged in conjunction with the trim control to rotate to the forward position on landing or to rotate backward on transition to horizontal flight. In the photo the seat is positioned in the horizontal flight position. Note the large handholds bolted to the windscreen's frame to help the pilot pull himself out of the cockpit when the aircraft is sitting on its tail.

At right top, the left pilot's console on the XFY-1 "Pogo". Notice that even though the seat is in the horizontal flight position, the armrests are in the vertical flight position. The seat switch is the lowest switch farthest to the right forward of the throttle. There are three small trim wheels mounted on the cockpit side behind the throttle control. These are from top to bottom, rudder, elevator, and aileron. The instruments in the upper right corner are left and right turbine temp. and left and right RPM,

At right bottom, right pilot's console. (all photos NASM)

around. These two mechanical functions were the trim switch and the seat switch. On one occasion I couldn't reach one of the switches right away, so we ganged these two switches so that trim and seat changes occurred at once when you hit the switch, which I think was about 100 mph.

CONCLUSION:

The Convair "pogo" project was a purely experimental project built around a experimental engine. The engine delivered all the power promised and was so powerful that at flight idle the XFY-1 would register 300 knots of airspeed. Our engine never gave us any trouble up until the end of the program when it was discovered that the gearbox was making metal. The lessons learned with the YT-40 helped develop the suc-cessful turboprops used on the C-130, P-3, and the Convair 580.

Progressive transition to horizontal flight as seen during the take off for the press on 4 November 1954. (National Archives)

"Skeets" Coleman coming back down for a landing on press day 4 November 1954 with a helicopter hovering at 100 feet. (via Long)

PRESS DEMONSTRATION 11-4-1954

Above, "Skeets" Coleman makes a high speed pass across the runway at NAAS Brown Field at about 75 feet. AD-5 chase plane is in the background. At right, XFY-1 kicks up a tremendous amount of dirt and debris during its descent to a perfect four-point landing. Below, safely on the ground, the ground crew rushes to help "Skeets" shut down the "Pogo". (National Archives)

Below, "Skeets" Coleman sitting in the cockpit after shutting down and completing the extremely successful press flight. The press and other dignitaries would go on to see a demonstration of the R3Y-1 "Tradewind" and the YF2Y-1 SeaDart (see Naval Fighters Number Twenty-Three, Convair XF2Y-1 and YF2Y-1 SeaDart). Note the Convair Logo is visible under the canopy as well as the open canopy latch. Also note cable system used to open and close the canopy and the location of the propeller decals on the underside of the lower propeller. (National Archives)

HORIZONTAL FLIGHT

Two views from below of a high speed pass at an altitude of about 75 feet. Even at idle the "Pogo" was traveling at a high rate of speed because of the extremely clean airframe and high performance 5,580 shaft horse power engine. The oleos for the four outrigger landing gear were fully extended even in horizontal flight. (National Archives)

At right, top, side view of XFY-1 during a high speed pass. (National Archives)

At right bottom, the XFY-1 at altitude during a horizontal flight assessing airflows and drag with tufting attached to the fuselage and wings. (via B. J. Long)

At left top and lower left, tethered flight rig set up on the concrete pad at NAAS Brown Field in May 1956. The lower fin tip and the left wing tip were covered with canvas. Note the red jet intake covers with red REMOVE BEFORE FLIGHT streamers attached. (National Archives)

At left lower right side, "Skeets" Coleman takes off on 1-28-55 at NAAS Brown Field. (via B. J. Long)

At right, "Skeets" passes over the desert at about 50 feet on 1-28-55. "Skeets" always flew the "Pogo" with the canopy open. (National Archives)

Below, prototype insulated steel and plywood covered "Tepee" type portable storage device as seen on 4-21-55. The structure provided a three level work platform for servicing the XFY-1 "Pogo". (National Archives)

RETIREMENT

Above and below, The XFY-1 "Pogo" on display on its decorated transporter at the August 1957 open house at NAS Miramar. Note VF-142 FJ-3 Furys in the background. (Clay Jansson)

At right, the "pogo" on outdoor display at NAS Norfolk on 6-1-67. (Clay Jansson)

Above, the XFY-1 in storage at Silver Hill in July 1986. Below, Close-up of the air intakes. At right, close-up of the exhaust.

"POGO" OBSERVATIONS BY WILLIAM F. "BILL" CHANA, FLIGHT TEST INSTRUMENTATION ENGINEER

My involvement in the "Pogo" was fairly minimal, I was a flight test engineer when "Skeets" was in flight test where we had a full scale "Pogo" mock-up that would transition from vertical to horizontal and back again. My responsibility was to design and install the test instrumentation on the "Pogo". I introduced "Skeets" to the "Pogo" mock-up prior to him volunteering for the program. We would sit in the cockpit and move the mock-up back and forth and while doing this we came up with the idea of putting a prone pilot capsule on the vertical fin tip to improve visibility. When the mock-up was in the vertical mode we could put a chair up against the tail and envision the benefits of a prone pilot position. One of the reasons we thought of this was because I had experience flying the "WeeBee" aircraft which had a prone flight position. From these thoughts we developed a patent proposal which we submitted to our patent department.

"Skeets" flew the aircraft very successfully because he had had some 60 hours of practice in the Moffett hanger where he could be captured if he got into trouble. He really had to learn how to fly all over again because the "Pogo" when in hover did not respond like a helicopter nor like an airplane. In the "Pogo" the rudder pedals moved the rudder, the lateral motion of the stick moved the aileron portion of the elevons, and the forward motion of the stick moved the elevator. So, when you put yourself in a hover the "Pogo" did not respond to the controls like a helicopter. In a helicopter if you want to move forward you move the stick forward, if you want to move aft you move the stick aft, if you want to move left you move the stick left, essentially if you want to move in any direction you point the stick in that direction and the helicopter moves in that direction. Well that's not the case in the "Pogo". In the "Pogo", yes you could move forward by moving the stick forward, if you wanted to go aft you could move the stick aft, however if you wanted to move to the left you had to move the rudder pedal. Now, if all you had to do was move forward and back or left and right, you might be able to pick that up in a hurry, but if you wanted to move off at 45° for example you would have to combine rudder and stick forces and really think about every move. It was very easy to become completely confused. Since "Skeets" had the benefit of the hanger training he was able to control the "Pogo". But when John Knebel tried it he didn't have the benefit of the tethered training and when you factor in the extreme throttle sensitivity that was needed you had a prescription for failure which very nearly happened on Knebal's vertical test flight. After the flight, I ran upstairs to the Corporate offices and told "Sparkey" Siebold, one of the VPs, you can't let anyone but "Skeets" fly that thing.

The interesting thing is we could have corrected that problem overnight so that anyone could have hovered it. That airplane had 100% hydraulic flight control systems and we could have just taken some hydraulic lines and moved them around and we could have made it so that the lateral motion of the stick would have moved the rudder, and the rudder pedals would have moved the aileron portion of the elevons. With that change anyone could have hovered it. Once you rotated into horizontal flight it would not have made any difference for a research plane. Because once your going 250 mph in level flight it doesn't matter if you kick in a little rudder or aileron the airplane will go in that direction. For a production airplane we could have developed a mixer box to transition the controls of the airplane to regular flight once it was horizontal.

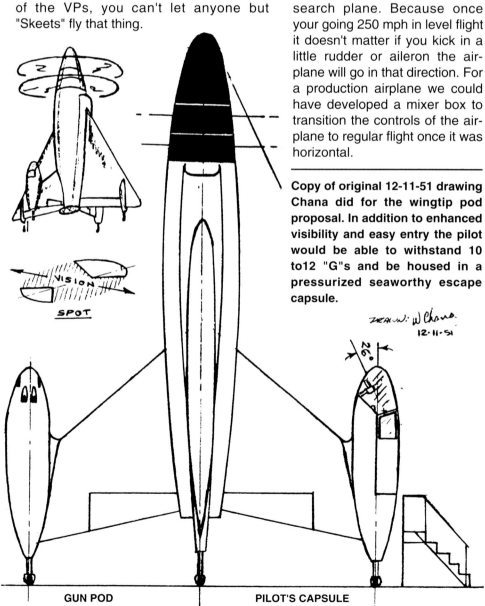

Copy of original 12-11-51 drawing Chana did for the wingtip pod proposal. In addition to enhanced visibility and easy entry the pilot would be able to withstand 10 to12 "G"s and be housed in a pressurized seaworthy escape capsule.

AIRMODEL VACUFORM KIT NUMBER 151

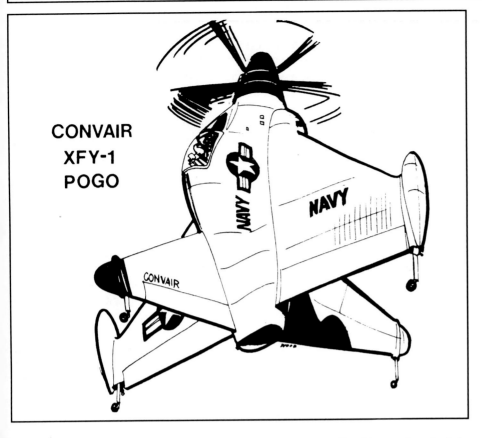

CONVAIR XFY-1 POGO

Airmodel produced it's 1/72 scale Pogo in the early 1970s. The kit consisted of six white and one clear vacuform parts. The model was built by R. J. Ferrara.

BILL CHANA'S VERNIER THROTTLE CONTROL PATENT STUDY FOR THE XFY-1

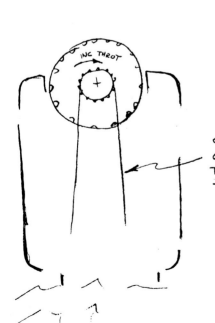

CABLE OR CHAIN DRIVE TO GEAR ON THROTTLE QUAD.

VERNIER
THROTTLE
QUADRANT

By: William F. Chana
DATE: July 10, 1951

NOTE:
THUMB CONTROLLED VERNIER THROTTLE WILL PROVIDE SMALL THROTTLE CHANGES WITH PROPER SENSE OF DIRECTION & COORDINATION CONSIDERED IMPORTANT IN HOVERING FLIGHT.

KP KIT NUMBER 33, THE 1/72 SCALE INJECTION MOULDED XFY-1 "POGO"

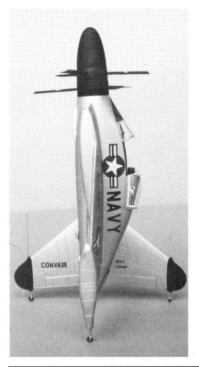

It was a big surprise when KP came out with a 1/72 scale injection moulded XFY-1 in late 1993. The kit is straight forward and easy to build. My only complaint is that the prop blades look to narrow to me on the completed model. The decal sheet was accurate except for the red on the stars-and-bars being off center. The decals included the proper Convair logo as displayed on the fuselage of the "Pogo".

THE LINDBERG 1/48 SCALE XFY-1 "POGO", KIT NUMBER 526 AND 536

The Lindberg "Pogo" was first issued in 1956 as kit number 526 and was offered with 23 injection moulded parts. The kit was updated with a boarding ladder in 1987 and consisted of 32 parts plus a bogus decal sheet. It makes up quite easily into a fairly accurate display model if you detail the cockpit from the spares box.